Pat the Penguin

By Sophie Reese Illustrated by Jackie Snider

Target Skill Consonant *Pp*/p/

PEARSON
Scott Foresman

penguin

I am Pat the penguin.

painter

I am a little painter.

popcorn

I like to have popcorn.

I am Pat the penguin.